I0021889

Windows 10

Get Ready for Windows 10 with this Complete Beginners Guide!

Table of Contents

Introduction

I want to thank you and congratulate you for downloading the book, "Windows 10: Get Ready for Windows 10 with this Complete Beginners Guide!"

This book contains proven steps and strategies on how to familiarize yourself with the "last version of Windows" regardless if you have already updated your system or you are still waiting for your queue.

After months of anticipation, Microsoft finally launched the Windows 10, which is a totally new version of the classic Windows operating system.

Although Windows 8.1 made some improvements, there's no denying that

Microsoft was complacent with Windows 8, probably perked up by the huge success of Windows 7. It was a product-centric approach with interface that was hard to learn and with features that didn't make any sense. To put it simply, Windows 8 is a failure, and Microsoft launched Windows 10 as a make or break product for the billion dollar company.

It is good that Windows 10 is quite different from Windows 8. Finally, Microsoft realized that users are willing to use other operating systems. The company now is keener on creating products for Linux, iOS, Android, and OS X. Also, it now allows apps from other platforms to be accessible through Windows.

Microsoft finally joined the modern idea of producing systems that can serve as a platform for all. Similar to Android, the current strength of Windows is in the thousands of third party companies that are developing apps for people to use in Windows. Hence, Windows 10 is no longer a mere OS for 32 and 54-bit personal computers. It will also operate on Advanced RISC Machine (ARM) platform for smartphones and tablets.

Apps will also run not only on PCS, but also on Windows phones, Xbox, and IoT devices.

Whether you have already upgraded to Windows 10 or still you still need to kick the tires, this book will serve as your guide in learning the basic features and some tips and tricks in using the Windows 10.

Thanks again for downloading this book, I hope you enjoy it!

Chapter 1 – Windows 10: The Last Version of Windows

Microsoft dubbed the Windows 10 as the "last version of Windows". This doesn't mean that the company will stop producing the Windows OS, but we might be saying goodbye to the concept of version numbers. We may not see a major upgrade or a huge launch every two to three years anymore. Similar to how Google updates the Chrome web browser regularly with version numbers that no one is paying attention to, the current strategy of Microsoft is geared towards that setting. This is the first step in considering Windows as a service and not as a product, and the idea that

Windows 10 is the last major version of Windows.

There's still the possibility that Microsoft may still choose to introduce Windows 11 or Windows 12 in the coming years, but if the company implement regular updates in the background while still running the OS, then users will just accept Windows without going through the hassle of upgrading to the latest version.

Upgrading to Windows 10

You can upgrade Windows 10 for free for the first year of release if your device is running on Windows 7 or Windows

8.1. If your device is running on Windows 7, Windows Vista, or Windows XP, you need to do a clean install and make certain that your device is compatible with the following system requirements:

- Microsoft account
- Internet access
- RAM: 1 gigabyte (GB) (32-bit) or 2 GB (64-bit)
- 1 gigahertz (GHz) or faster
- 16 GB available free hard disk space
- Graphics card: Microsoft DirectX 9 graphics device with WDDM driver

Although the free upgrade version of

Windows 10 is available for this year, Microsoft assured that those who are upgrading during its promotional period will still be able to use the OS for free forever or as the company ensures lifetime support of the device. Once you update, you will be upgraded to the proper versions.

Versions of Windows 10

There will be seven versions of Windows 10. These are Home, Mobile, Professional, Enterprise, Mobile Enterprise, Education and Internet of Things (IoT). The latter is suitable for devices like Intel Galileo, Raspberry Pi, and Creator Ci20 of Imagination. Windows 10 Mobile and Mobile

Enterprises are designed for smartphones and tablets with sizes less than eight inches.

Windows 10 Home has consumer features such as Cortana and Windows Hello that you can use for logging into your computer using a face recognition system or fingerprint scanner. Windows 10 Mobile is fun to use. Instead of Internet Explorer, it features the new Microsoft Edge. Mobile Enterprise resembles the interface of Windows 10 Enterprise but for smaller screens.

The Professional and Enterprise versions come with management and security upgrades. It also has a new way for licensing, which includes the capacity to sign in using the Azure Active Directory accounts. Both versions can join in the domain.

Also included in Windows 10 Professional are BitLocker disk encryption, Remote Desktop, business version of Windows Store, and the assigned access that enables you to lock your PC to run only like a modem app to be used similar to a kiosk. Network administrators can also set aside specific time for updates so they will not happen when you are using the PC for important stuff.

Windows Enterprise also includes a group of policy Direct Access, which allows you to connect even without a Virtual Private Network or VPN, BranchCache to share downloads, and the AppLocker to whitelist applications.

Windows 10 Education, as the name suggests, is suited for educational institutions like colleges, universities, research facilities, and the like. The interface is similar to Windows 10 Enterprise, but it can also be added as a Home upgrade. Hence, schools can link student devices to their own PCs.

Microsoft offers support for whatever version of Windows 10 you get until

2020 with extended support until 2025.

If you are running a Windows version that is suitable for upgrade, you will see an icon appearing on the desktop through the Windows Update. This will only appear if your device is compatible for the upgrade. Clicking this icon will launch a window, which will allow you to reserve your place on queue to be able to download Windows 10.

When you upgrade, you will lose some features that you have on Windows, but they are good riddance such as Media Center, desktop gadgets from Vista, and Windows 8 Metro.

Chapter 2 – Changes and Improvements in Windows 10

Windows 10 has a complete new interface and look that has the best features from Windows 7, some from Windows 8, and a load of new options. As a matter of fact, so much have changed that from the moment you turn on your PC to the moment you shut it down, you need to work in new ways to get stuff done.

Windows 10 runs on desktops, laptops, tablets, smartphones, and other forms of computing devices. Instead of enumerating these devices every time we are talking about the OS, let's just simply say your device. Whenever you read it, we are talking about all the different forms of devices that can run on Windows 10.

Welcome Back, Start Menu

The user interface has been significantly improved in Windows 10. Fortunately, Microsoft restored the Start Menu. Its interface is similar to the Windows 7 and has some features from Windows 8. Also added is a notification sidebar, and you can change its look according to your device. Users were not satisfied with Windows 8, so Microsoft identified the need for a new OS, which improves on the pitfalls of the previous version.

It's easy to scroll down through the Live Tiles, which are also animated. The tiles will rotate if there are fresh content that you may want to check out. Just like with Windows 8, you can group and rename the live tiles. You can also resize the start menu by dragging the sides, but you cannot switch the live tiles totally off.

In the Insider version, many users complained that the live tiles on the Start Menu are not good enough. But with the launched version, users are looking at the live tiles as they animate. Many have found some interesting updates like news and weather. The live tiles are very useful for at-a-glance things.

The rest of the Start Menu is similar to the Windows 7, with controls to restart, sleep, or shutdown the PC. There are also apps and the ability to scroll down through the applications alphabetically via the All Apps menu. Also present are the Settings and File Explorer.

Action Center

All the previous Charms features are now located in the Action Center, which is an improved Notifications panel. You can launch this from the notifications area on the taskbar. Once you open the Action Center a full-height bar will appear on the right, which is designed like the Notifications setup in the Windows Phone.

Network Menu

The new network menu allows you to easily access the network settings. You just need to click on the network icon on the taskbar. Aside from accessing the network settings, you can also switch between these settings.

Text Input Canvas

The text input canvas has been considerably enhanced in Windows 10. The manner that to provide the input text has been improved, and this is designed for tablets and smartphones. Similar to the movements on smartphone keyboards, handwriting can be recognized and also includes predictive text.

Controls are located on the right panel, which helps you to delete words or to return to a letter as well as to choose the types of available keywords. The area for writing has a more compact design compared to the previous version.

Windows Cortana

Cortana is a smart personal assistant, first introduced in Windows Phone. It can help you find things in your device, find files, manage your calendars, define words, update you on weather and the latest news, and even sing you a song or tell you jokes. Cortana will learn more about you use it to improve your user experience.

You can type your question in the search box on the taskbar, or you can choose the mic icon and talk to Cortana.

Here are some things you can say to Cortana:

- Show me the latest news.

- Who is Barack Obama?

- What is the meaning of bucolic?

- Show me the latest FIFA scores

- Remind me about the PTA meeting tomorrow

- How many calories are there in a pepperoni pizza?

- Open Microsoft Word

- What's my schedule today?

Enhanced Virtual Desktops

Windows 10 offers the improved version of Virtual Desktops. They are numbered, and you can drag and drop between several desktops. The current desktop you are presently working on will show the icons, which are open on the taskbar.

In the early versions of Windows 10, the Action Center was still a work in progress, but now it is usable and powerful. A selection of individual settings (referred to as Quick Actions) is located at the bottom of the Action Center. These have been standard for Android and iOS in toggling Wi-Fi, Bluetooth, and it's great that Windows also have them. You can also access the Settings here (aside from the Start Menu), and switch to Tablet mode. The Note feature has also been added so you can easily launch OneNote.

As you will notice, there are also other features to control connectivity like the ability to link devices like Bluetooth speakers. For smartphones and tablets, you can also toggle rotation. Another new feature is Quiet Hours that will banish all notifications on specific times that you don't want to be disturbed.

Microsoft Edgc

Previously known as Project Spartan, Microsoft Edge is the new browser for

Windows 10, permanently replacing Internet Explorer. In the final version of Windows 10, Microsoft Edge considerably improved and can be used as a browser.

The Default Home Page of the Microsoft Edge is simple, interesting, and inviting. The clean home page will ask you "Where to next?" on top of the integrated search and address bar. Under that are links to popular websites, and under that is the information feed that features customized news based on your Microsoft Account. Of course, the built in search is powered by Bing.

Edge also features other cool stuff such as the Reading List, which allows you to save webpages and articles for later reading similar to Instapaper or Pocket, but you need to be online. Edge could present a web page in a simplified format, which removes the banners and ads for easier reading. The note-taking feature also allows you to mark up or doodle or write directly on the web page, then save the image to OneNote or share it through another app.

Enhanced Virtual Desktops

Windows 10 offers the improved version of Virtual Desktops. They are numbered, and you can drag and drop between several desktops. The current desktop you are presently working on will show the icons, which are open on the taskbar.

In the early versions of Windows 10, the Action Center was still a work in progress, but now it is usable and powerful. A selection of individual settings (referred to as Quick Actions) are located at the bottom of the Action Center. These have been standard for Android and iOS in toggling Wi-Fi, Bluetooth, and it's great that Windows also have them. You can also access the Settings here (aside from the Start Menu), and switch to Tablet mode. The Note feature has also been added so you can easily launch OneNote.

As you will notice, there are also other features to control connectivity like the ability to link devices like Bluetooth speakers. For smartphones and tablets, you can also toggle rotation. Another new feature is Quiet Hours that will banish all notifications on specific times that you don't want to be disturbed.

Taskbar

There are no significant changes in the taskbar, but the opened apps are added with a subtle color under them, while the improved Search bar that you can minimize to an icon or eliminate totally through the taskbar. Task View icons are still present, near the Start button.

As you will also notice, the Windows logo also got smaller as the development went on. The interface of the Notifications area on the right end is now much simpler with the addition of the Action Center. The App icons can be accessed via pop-up, and you can drag them in and out for access.

The calendar has been improved. Just click on the clock icon to access it and change the date and time settings. Now you can again minimize everything when you click the right hand corner of the taskbar.

File Explorer Improvements

File Explorer has undergone some

enhancements. Quick Access has been added where you can add or delete any folder that you want to easily access. In the Home screen, you can also access the Frequent Folders and Recent Files, which can help you to navigate through your files easily. You can add folders to the Quick Access permanently by right clicking their icon and choosing the Add to Quick Access option.

You will also notice that different icons have changed - most of them have gone through several improvements since the Insider Version of Windows 10. A lot more file operations have been added that you can choose on the top ribbon without the need to right click the icons.

OneDrive is also integrated within the File Explorer. Although it is now part of the operating system, it will not affect your tasks if you do away with it.

The Windows Store and the Universal Apps

Windows 10 made a lot of improvement when it comes to built-in and third-party applications. Microsoft now adapts the concept of Universal Apps in its target to encourage developers to build their apps not only for PC but also for Mobile and Xbox.

These Universal Apps replaced the Modern UI apps or Metro apps that were present in the Windows 8 and 8.1.

These are different to desktop apps, but they can also be accessed in the desktop and they also have Live Tile options in the Start Menu.

It is clear that Microsoft wants to rectify its error with Windows 8 when it assumed that app developers will use the new OS. Hence, it is now easier for developers to convert current apps running in Android, while they can use the Microsoft Visual Studio 2015 to create iOS apps and run them as Universal apps in PC.

The Windows Store has also been improved with its revamped design and selections for Universal Apps and desktop apps.

Similar to Universal apps, the desktop apps installed using the Windows Store will be managed from there. So they will easily install after clicking the install or download button once. After installation, they will be sandboxed in the Universal apps area.

Developers can use the App-V (Application Virtualization) to prepare their apps to run in the Windows Store. Tech companies can also launch apps from their own Windows Store and managed from the Business Store Portal that handles centralized payment info, software licenses and more.

Chapter 3 – Security Features in Windows 10

Biometric authentication and application-vetting underscore the new primary security features in Windows 10. The security features of Windows 10 integrated with the new Windows Store for vetted and authorized apps, Microsoft is building the desktop ecosystem to look a lot more in the smartphone. This is a good thing for security.

Microsoft Device Guard

The primary function of the new Microsoft Device Guard is to prevent attacks by apps that are trying to access your device and its network. It will block any app that is not authorized by certain software vendors and the Windows app.

Manufacturers such as Acer, HP, Fujitsu, Par, Toshiba, and Lenovo have partnered with Microsoft to use Device Guard on their devices that are running on Windows. It also provides support for ATM machines, point-of-sale systems, and other IoT-type devices that are running on Windows.

In order to protect your device from malware once the app is executed, Windows will determine if the app is trustworthy, and will notify you if it fails the trust test. Device Guard uses virtualization and hardware technology to isolate that feature from the main OS, which helps in protecting the device from malware that aims to obtain full system privilege.

It is also interesting to take note that Device Guard also virtually operates so that even if the kernel is under attack and compromised, the Device Guard will be isolated.

Windows Hello

Windows Hello is a new feature that uses biometrics - your iris, fingerprint, or face - to start your device instead of using vulnerable passwords. This feature makes the device more secure because it lets you authenticate apps, online experiences, and enterprise content without the need to store a password on the network server or the device.

However, your device requires a fingerprint reader function and scanning software and hardware so it can identify the user by his iris or face. The device also requires Windows Biometric Framework Support.

The OEM systems that incorporate the Intel RealSense 3D Camera will support the facial recognition technology of Windows Hello, which includes automatic sign in to Windows.

Passport

Another security feature that is consistent with the password-free authentication is the Windows Passport, which allows you to authenticate websites, networks, and apps without using passwords.

Windows 10 will request you to authenticate that you are actually using the device before proceeding with the authentication on your behalf using the Windows Hello or your own PIN. After being authenticated with Passport, you can access an increasing set of services and websites such as frequently visited websites, social networking platforms, email, online banking services, business networks, and many more.

Passport works with the Azure Active Directory Services and your biometric signature will be secured and stored within the device and will be used to unlock the device.

However, Microsoft is not imposing the demise of passwords, even though now as member of the FIDO Alliance, the company is now working to replace passwords in the future. So if you are comfortable in using password, you don't need to use Windows Hello and Passport at all.

Microsoft also made some subtle yet crucial changes in Windows 10 by using virtualized sandboxes and containers to help in improving the security of desktops.

Chapter 4 – Tips and Tricks in Using Windows 10

Now that you know the new features and improvements on the interface and security in Windows 10, it's now time to look at some of the tips, tricks, and hidden features of the OS.

Voice Command Your PC

Cortana's integration to the PC is one of the best features of Windows 10. Now you can assume control of the search functions of the OS. But by default, Cortana doesn't listen to your instructions.

If you prefer to control your PC just by using your own voice, you simply open Cortana by clicking the search field beside the Start Menu and choose the Notebook icon on the left panel. Choose Settings from the list, and just turn on the option "Let Cortana respond when you say 'Hey Cortana'" Make sure that you have an active microphone for this feature to work.

When you are browsing around the options for Cortana, you can poke into the Notebook menu to customize the data that Cortana can access. Bear in mind that similar to Google Now, the efficiency of Cortana depends on how much information she knows.

Your digital assistant can handle will many types of commands using natural language such as adding reminders, playing music, or updating you on the weather (as discussed in Chapter 2). However, the most powerful use of its ability to recognize natural language revolves around basic search options. For example, you can instruct Cortana to "Find files created in August" or "Find excel files" and she will apply the proper filters, then browse your local files and storage to give you results.

Personalize Your Start Menu

Now you can personalize the Start menu. If you are comfortable with the integration of conventional interface with the Live Tiles, you can easily resize the tile's dimensions similar to the Start screen in the Windows 8. But if you don't like Live Tiles, you can also right click on each live tile and choose Uninstall to delete them from the OS. An alternative is to simply unpin them from the Start Menu or hide them. Add the software or apps you want to use, by right clicking any program and choosing Pin to start option.

Customize Your Mail

Microsoft made a lot of improvements in the latest version of its Mail and Calendar in comparison to the offerings in Windows 8. These apps open quickly, added with full features, and more user friendly. The new Mail also comes with customization options that allow you to personalize the app. You can change the picture in the preview pane with your chosen image, and you can also change the behavior of the Mail with new swipe gestures.

Schedule Updates

If you have pending updates that require to start your PC, the new OS will let you schedule a particular time to do so. You just need to access the Settings option in the Start menu, then find the Updates and Recovery and Windows Update. You can also browse around the advanced options and ask Windows to remind you to schedule the restart once updates are ready to roll off.

You can also get Windows Update from other sources. Microsoft now allows the option to download updates from peer-to-peer sites instead of directly downloading the updates from Microsoft. This will enable you to obtain the hot security patch easier when other users are still on queue to download the updates from Microsoft servers. This will also allow you to save on bandwidth in an organization. You just need to download a new patch from Microsoft, then share it through the internal network.

Record Video Apps

The new Game DVR feature of Windows 10 is mainly designed to record videos of your most exciting game moments. However, it can also be used to record videos of any app or software that you are using.

To enable this function, just press Windows key and G. There will be a prompt that will ask if you want to access the Game bar. Just click yes, and different options will appear. Enable the record button to capture a video. You can find the saved videos in the Game DVR section of the Xbox app.

Solitaire is back

After being deleted in Windows 8, Solitaire returns in Windows 10. You can enjoy it as long as you know where to find it. It's not in the Start Menu, and even searching for t in the All Apps section is also futile. The game is named as Microsoft Solitaire Collection Preview. Just search for it in all apps, and it will just appear.

Chapter 5 – Common User Problems with Windows 10

Since its launch in July 29, the response to Windows 10 has been astoundingly positive. Certainly, this new OS from Microsoft seems like a considerable improvement when you compare it to Windows 8, which was negatively received by users.

It appears that people love the comeback of the Start Menu replacing the Start screen that no one likes, and new features such as Edge web browser and Cortana are main features that users love.

But of course, there are still issues that users encounter in using Windows 10. Even with positive response, there are still bumps on the road. Below are some of the common problems you may face, and if available, some tips you can do to fix the issue.

Reservation

Because the OS update is being sent in waves, not all users can qualify for the update. Windows Insiders are entitled to receive the update first, followed by users who have already reserved a spot directly from Microsoft. Take note that you cannot reserve for the update unless your system is already running Windows 8.1 or Windows 7 SP1. Your device should also be compatible with the system requirements as discussed in Chapter 1.

Post-Installation Activation Issues

Some users are complaining about the difficulty in activating Windows 10 after installation. There's really nothing you can do to fix this, because it will usually resolve itself after several minutes.

Forced Updates

Windows 10 will not give you an option in updating your system, it will immediately accepts them even without your permission. In the pro column, automatic updates can help your device to run smoothly by making certain that its system is updated in security patches. However, automatic update will enable Microsoft to force-feed virtually anything it wants into your device. You can't fix this unless you are using Windows 10 Enterprise which allows you to accept or deny system updates.

Another issue caused by the automatic updates is that it can cause your device to crash. A reboot can fix this on a case by case basis, and you can also choose to uninstall the driver that is causing the issue.

Chrome Has Gone Slow

In using Chrome web browser, users have experienced several problems such as slow browsing and bog downs, specifically if they are using bandwidth heavy tasks such as video streaming. You have to wait for Google to fix down the bugs, but you can try deleting your extensions in the meantime, or try reinstalling Chrome.

Printer not responding

If after the update you notice that your printer is not working properly, you may need to restart the whole installation process. To ensure smooth connectivity, you need to update everything including the drivers before the upgrade. Also make certain that you are using a printer that is compatible with Windows.

Folder Errors

Based on user reports, there is actually one aspect where Windows 8 is better compared to Windows 10. The new email app will not allow you to create subfolders when you need to organize your email. For this user, this is a major issue, and for the time being, there is still no way to fix this.

Connectivity Glitch

There are users who filed complaint about issues when they are trying to connect with Wi-Fi. This is actually a common problem in most versions of Windows, and you can fix this by restarting your device. You can also try to disable Wi-Fi sharing to stabilize the connection.

Conclusion

Thank you again for downloading this book!

I hope this book was able to help you to familiarize yourself with the new features and improvements with Windows 10.

The next step is to update your system if you haven't already done so, and enjoy the exciting features of this new operating system from Microsoft.

Finally, if you enjoyed this book, then I'd like to ask you for a favor, would you be kind enough to leave a review for this book on Amazon? It'd be greatly appreciated!

Thank you and good luck!

www.ingramcontent.com/pod-product-compliance
Lightning Source LLC
Chambersburg PA
CBHW070900070326
40690CB00009B/1921